Phases of a Butterfly:
The Caterpillar

SHUNTONESE RICHARDSON

Phases of a Butterfly by Shuntonese Richardson

Published by The SNR Collection & SNR Publishing LLC

Chicago Il.

www.thesnrcollection.com

© 2020 Shuntonese Richardson

All rights reserved. No portion of this book may be reproduced in any form without permission from the publisher, except as permitted by U.S. copyright law. For permissions contact: shuntonesetheauthor@yahoo.com

Graphic Designer:Jason McFarling

Printed in United States

2 Edition

Disclaimer: This book contains vulgar language which may be offensive to some readers and/or inappropriate for children. Reader discretion is advised.

PHASES OF A BUTTERFLY: THE CATERPILLAR

I collaborated with God to make this...

When you stay faithful, focused and consistent,
God has a way of clearing your path.
He will make the road easy for you.
But you have to be willing to do the work
WHILE believing.

PHASES OF A BUTTERFLY: THE CATERPILLAR

Feb 9, 2021
GROUNDED.
Just trying to find balance.

I didn't start winning until I started working on myself.
Focusing on me.
Loving solely on myself.
No more compromising me for them.
No more.
It's my turn.
It's my time.

PHASES OF A BUTTERFLY: THE CATERPILLAR

When I started walking in the light of who God called me
to be,
My path got clearer
and quite easier.
There's no confusion.
My plans are laid out in front of me,

I just have to execute.

"Respond instead of React"
It is such a powerful statement
And really just ate me up.
Whole.

I'm like a firecracker
and not the kind you light
and then as it gets shorter
It explodes.
I'm the one you just throw on the ground
And I pop
So be careful how you handle me.

Working on my anger and my mouth
is the hardest part of my journey.
Knowing my battles and what's worth responding or
reacting to is a hard hill to get over.
When you take the time to respond,
It's calculated.
Thought through.
When you react,
It's based on emotions
And emotions change.

I once heard a saying something like
"give it 24-48 hours and if you still feel the same way, then
react. If not, let it go"
.. and I completely agree.
Sometimes trauma forces our emotions to react before we
truly process what's going on.
Most things aren't even worth responding to or giving our
energy to.
But trauma makes us think otherwise.

PHASES OF A BUTTERFLY: THE CATERPILLAR

I'm always nervous when it's time to start something new
or do something I've never done.
For example:
Going to a job interview or the first day of school or work..
My anxiety flares up really bad.
I get so anxious that I make excuses not to go.

I haven't found any ways to cope with my anxiety just yet.

The doctors say meds,
but I'm not a crackhead.
My friends say a therapist.
Is it weird that I only want a black therapist?
Black and female.
Someone who really understands,
not the kind who grew up in the suburbs
with both parents
who gave her a car for her sweet sixteen
She can't relate to me.
I went to 7-8 schools by the time I graduated out of high school.
My parents are still causing trauma to me,
and I'm going on 24.
I rode the bus to school
and had to stay at friends' houses.
I bought my own car with the help of my mom,
and I had my first apartment at 19.
I need someone who understands that life is hard,
and I'm just using what I was given to get where I want.

Dealing with family drama is wild to me.
Having issues with your parents is so left field.
I've always looked at other people's family dynamic with envy.
I've always wished I was born into a family with the basics
The love
The support
The norm
I really don't even like to discuss my views on my family.
because I don't feel it's worth it.
But for me to grow into the woman I'm meant to be,
I can only assume it'll be needed one day.
to talk about how it's hindered me.
and my relationship-making skills with others.
The disconnect I feel between me and other humans,
especially men
is deeply rooted in that childhood trauma.

When the word trauma is used
it usually denotes something awful.
I don't think I had an awful childhood.
I actually think I had a great upbringing.
But getting older and looking deeper,
there were a lot of problems there that weren't ever addressed
or ever talked about that affected me greatly.

PHASES OF A BUTTERFLY: THE CATERPILLAR

Allowing people to half love you
and still claim you love yourself
is a myth.
It's a belief that is inaccurate.
I use to believe that I loved myself

but I just let other people love me roguishly.
That itself says that I can't possibly love me
If I allow other people to mistreat, hurt
Or disrespect me
That's not love.

SHUNTONESE RICHARDSON

A sad reality for me is that
I never felt seen.
Only
tolerated
because of what I had to offer.

I was always beneficial.
Never felt.
Only what I can do for people.

Love in this generation is so transactional.

"Ain't it funny how life goes around? The same people you meet going up, you'll see them coming down." - Heather Headley

"Trauma bonding is when you're so
heavily attached to a toxic person,
that you are willing to maintain a relationship,
even at the expense of yourself
for the few and far between highs.
Your brain gets highly addicted to
the habitual ups and downs of oxytocin,
dopamine-makes you crave them more.
You're dependent in the same way a heroin addict is."

PHASES OF A BUTTERFLY: THE CATERPILLAR

Soul tie.
How can something live in my spirit,
Untangleable actually
be physically tied
to another body?
Why do I feel so deeply?
Why can't I let go?
Who tied this?
Who agreed to this?
Are soul ties meant to be for good?
Why does this feel so painful?

I thought I was strong enough to heal him.
But he literally sucked me dry.
You never want to give so much that it leaves you empty.
That's not love.
Because then what/who will fill you back up if you can't?
Who will comfort you?
Never humble yourself…
The love you give.
Your spirit.
Your sense of being.
To be someone else's.

Be yours first.

Be you,
for you

first.

Would you ever want your daughter to be you?
silenced and hushed
because she's too scared of hurting
or losing another person,
that she can't be herself
or say what she feels?
If the answer is no,
change your situation.

Live in your truth.
Love in your language.

PHASES OF A BUTTERFLY: THE CATERPILLAR

October 26th, 2021
How can you do something bold to me and fuck up my trust in you?
Then be mad that I have my guard up?

Manipulation at its best.

But it doesn't work for me.

I'm not perfect
what so ever
but since I've met you, I just wanted to be better.
I want to be loved
and show love.
Even after you've told me multiple times that's not what
you wanted.
And that's on me
I just really couldn't fight it.
You made me feel...
different.
Though, I've pictured myself being your wife.
But I've shown my hand
and you've shown yours.
You've done what you needed to do to protect yourself at
our time of compromise
and now it's time I stand on my own boundaries
and do what's best for me.
Maybe we will meet again
and/or can be friends later on
but right now I just don't know.
It's not good for my journey
or my mental health.
You're an amazing person,
and I really did see a future with you
but you're just not the person destined for me.
You've taught me a lot about myself
and challenged the greatest parts of me
and I appreciate that.
I'm letting you go,
humbly

PHASES OF A BUTTERFLY: THE CATERPILLAR

and gracefully
and I hope it's nothing but love on your end!

I'm really not good at "letting go" once in love
and this is extremely hard for me.
But I know I need to make better choices as I grow into
the woman I'm supposed to be.
And those choices end this.

This is goodbye.

SHUNTONESE RICHARDSON

I always write the most,
when I feel the most.

Thanks for making me feel something.

Sometimes I wish I had some of the hard-core traits this generation has.
Grimey, Sneaky, and Selfish.
People with those traits go through life with no worries.
Like karma doesn't exist.
I no longer step out of who I've become to prove myself or even get my lick back.
Between karma and God, no on who has ever done be wrong
Ended up in a better position than me.
I can guarantee that.

I can't even do people bogus without feeling it.
I always pride myself in moving well and with pure intentions.

That's how I sleep at night.

You can't talk about things you want to happen
prematurely,
which is really sad.
Evil eyes are real and jealousy is creeping through the
veins of even your closest mates.
People will prey on and against you secretly but smile in
your face.
Learning to keep my goals to myself until they are fully
complete
and to stop sharing them prematurely
because some people could be secretly praying against
you.
People always want to see you doing good,
never on the same level or further than them.
That's actually contradictory because you're supposed to
be able to tell your circle everything.
But these days, you'll never know who secretly despises
you.

Protect you.
Protect your goals.
Protect your dreams
Protect your energy.

This year I want to grow out of prioritizing people
who don't prioritize me.
And not stress it.
If they wanted to,
they would.

Learning to love who loves me.

One thing about pretending,

you can only pretend so long.

PHASES OF A BUTTERFLY: THE CATERPILLAR

"You gotta find out who you dealing with... and fuck with them on their level"
Atlanta 2020

When you ask God to remove people,
do not invite them back no matter how much you miss them!

PHASES OF A BUTTERFLY: THE CATERPILLAR

Nothing you're meant to have, will have to be forced. Worked hard for, MAYBE..

but NEVER forced.

Don't ever let anyone make you feel like
you should be worthy of even a second
of their presence.
You are
and were worthy in your own world
before it all!
God deemed you 1 of 1!
Don't ever forget it!

People only know how to be there for you,
when it's convenient for them.
If they aren't happy at the moment
or not in their winning season
they aren't checking on you to see how you are.
Because it's not convenient for them.
Be careful about conditional people.
Watch out for
"if it benefits me then I can be here".
Be mindful of those who are always around in their or
your winning season,
but never around to buy you an umbrella when the
storms come.
Stay clear.
Weed them out.
You need people around that no matter what page of life
you're on,
they are still there.
Let harsh tides wash away those who are easily swayed.
We don't need any loopholes in this next season!
We don't need the unsure,
the disloyal
or the questionable.

You're either riding or you're not. No discussion!

Dealing with anxiety is a crazy ride.
It feels like you're in a dark room.
And you can feel the water growing.
First your feet, then your legs.
Now your knees
then your hips.
Now the waters to your shoulders
and you're struggling to stand on your tippy toes.
The water is starting to fill your mouth
and lungs
and soon it'll be so high you won't be able to see above it.
You black out.

All while just sitting in your car.
Or the front of your shop.
Or the living room floor.

Anxiety is cold.
Lonely.
Big.
Anxiety makes you forget the reality of what's going on.
The thoughts consume you and trick your mind and body
into believing that it's over for you.
But it's all in your mind.
It's literally all in your mind.

Go to your happy place.
Find your safe place.
Breathe.
Slow and steady, in and out.
Breathe.

What's your name?
Who are you?
And not the you-anxiety is trying to make you believe you are.
Who are you really?
What makes you, you?
What's your favorite color?
Or your favorite song in the morning?
What do you do on a Sunday morning or Tuesday night that reminds you that you are good?

You're still you.
Perfectly imperfect but still you.
You're that good. You're that smart. You're that witty.
You're that brave. You're that strong.

Remember?
Don't let anxiety force you into a corner and make you feel small.

Come home,
please.

Healing from losing a loved one is like a roller coaster ride.
Some days are good.
While others are so heavy you want to leave too.
You'll be good, feeling okay.
Smiling and getting into the groove of things then boom……
The song on the radio reminds you of them
or their favorite team just won the playoffs.
Now you can't stop the tears from falling.

Sometimes the weight is so heavy you can't get out of bed,
or be a mom,
or a friend,
or even you.

The pain is so strong
it weighs you down.

You feel so low.

Grief feels like an elephant sitting on your chest.

PHASES OF A BUTTERFLY: THE CATERPILLAR

Suicide is tough.
The person feels like they don't have any other options.
But they do.
They always do.
I would say suicide is selfish
but that's selfish in itself.

I can say
suicide is a one sided theory.

If for a second you feel like you don't have anything to live for,
think of that one person that wouldn't be the same
if you weren't here anymore.
No matter how much of a burden,
one may feel,
They are someone's smile on a bad day.
Someone's breath of fresh air.
Someone else's reason to continue.

There is always a reason to stay.
So please decide to stay.

Find your reason.
And if ever you feel like you can't find one,

Be one!

The devil is riding me hard.
He wants me badly
Hurdle
after hurdle
Hardship
after hardship.
He wants me to give up so badly.

BUT THAT'S TOO DAMN BAD.

I am God's daughter.
One of his favorites, actually.
I am fully covered in his love.
From the top of my head
to the bottom of my toes.

The devil can't have me.
I'm sorry.

I'm taken already, love.

Under heavy fire and being tested like crazy.
God wants to know how I'll handle things
When nothing is under my control.
When nothing is in my favor.
Especially when I feel like I did nothing wrong.

Will I sink or fly?
Fall or prevail?

I don't know,
All I know is that my faith in God is
bigger.

So I know I have to show God He can trust me.

SHUNTONESE RICHARDSON

Control what you can
and don't worry about anything outside of that.

PHASES OF A BUTTERFLY: THE CATERPILLAR

A lot of people always want to know about my spinal surgery.
And why I was so quiet during that time.
I was quiet because I wasn't aware of my feelings then.

I was only 21,
Broken back,
temporarily paralyzed,
and pregnant.
There was not much for me to say, honestly.
I was sad
and ashamed.
I was embarrassed.
My life was dark.
My world was dark.
My thoughts were dark.
I couldn't see past the fog.

To the people who did know
and held my hand through it,
Thank you.
You guys were my reason.

I often talk about
how I never planned to have kids so early,
and how the only reason I decided against it
was because it was the only thing I really had.
He was the only thing I had.

He is my light.
During the late nights

when all my family was gone,
the lights were off
and visiting time was over,
all I had was this baby's heart beat
and God's Grace.

I did not know what I'd do with a child.
especially under the circumstances.
No car,
I didn't have a place to live of my own.
I barely had a job.
But I vowed that if God let me out of bed
and gave me another chance to get up and walk
I'd give this world the best I had to offer.
I'd be the best mommy I could be.

And I did.
And I still am.

I'm not perfect,
In any aspect.
But I give this world 110% everyday,
because I have a purpose.
I'm meant to be here.

And I'm here to stay.

Everything that I've gone against has made me stronger.

RESILIENT.
Tailor made.
God touched.

It's 2:22am March 10th, 2022

I'm actually up because my son is getting over the flu, so
we haven't been sleeping.
But I'd figure I'd tell it.

March 10th, 2018 —
changed my life forever.
I was in a car accident in which the doctors said
had I not been in the seat belt
I would have died.
BUT MY GOD HAD OTHER PLANS FOR ME.
I was hospitalized
with immediate surgery:
A broken back
and a gash on my forehead.

You've heard people say
"life flashed before my eyes"
and I literally lived that moment.

As my car struck the pole,
I could feel life slowing down and my last thoughts were
"I'm never about to die like this."
BUT GOD HAD OTHER PLANS FOR ME.

I had to relearn to walk
and pee
and do all my daily tasks on my own again.
I used to sit and ask God-
How did this become my life?

What did I do wrong?

I hid what happened to me for so long.
I was HURT
embarrassed
and ashamed.

But over time
I started to understand
that God needed to show me what the bottom looked
like
So I'll be grateful for mountain tops
when I see them!

So when you see me never complaining
and working my butt off-
This is why.

GOD HAS FAVORED ME
AND GAVE ME TOO MANY CHANCES TO NOT
MAKE THIS LIFE COUNT.
God is a forgiving God
He's a faithful God.

I don't cry about raindrops because I've been through
storms bigger than my mind, body and my spirit!!!

I'm grateful to have God.
The people who have always held my hand through this
life and hopefully the next,
and strength within myself

to push beyond the break.

It took me months to get back.
I did have to wear a body cast
but I was determined.
I was determined to show God
that He didn't make a mistake with me.

And God willing,

today on my crash anniversary
I can walk normally and function in everyday life
like this incident never happened.
WHERE DOCTORS SAID TEMPORARILY
PARALYZED,
GOD SAID "GET UP BABY GIRL I GOT YOU"

I don't throw this story or my story around because I'm
never looking for pity.
But I've learned to let my testimony use me.

AS LONG AS YOU HAVE BREATH IN YOUR
BODY,
a few good people around
and faith in GOD…
YOU CAN COME BACK FROM ANYTHING!!!!

Believe me.

Thank you God for where I am right now.
Today.
May 13th, 2021
1:55pm.
Today is EID.
And I'm just taking it all in.
I'm grateful for what's to come
and thankful for all that I have lost in the works to get here.
I am overjoyed about all that my God has let me take on:
the wins
and losses,
made the journey.
Made me, ME.

May not be perfect,
but it was worth every door that's about to open for me!

Thank you God,
for my yesterday
that made today shine
and tomorrow something to look forward to.

No regrets,
pick up the lessons
and GO.
If things had not happened the way they did,
you wouldn't be where you are.
The knowledge,
the experience,
the strength,
would all be gone.
Take what you gained
and MOVE.

But now you'll move a bit smarter
and wiser.

No regrets.
Go!

PHASES OF A BUTTERFLY: THE CATERPILLAR

It's never about whether my glass is half empty or full,
more so, thankful for the quality of the glass.
Life isn't about weeding out the good or the bad
But being grateful for the journey in itself.

Today at school, my teacher said
"What's wrong, are you ok?"
And I replied;
"No, how do you know?"
and she said "it's all in your eyes"

YOUR EYES NEVER LIE.

My eyes are my favorite trait,

always have been.

PHASES OF A BUTTERFLY: THE CATERPILLAR

Feeling everything at once has got to be a crime.

Either feeling everything or nothing at all
is a hard choice to make.
but I always choose the latter of the two.

I don't know,
I'll just rather not be attached to anything.
No worries,
no tears,
no weakness.
Or is that my weakness?

Not being able to attach is beginning to seem undesirable
as I get older.

Move more intentionally,
With purpose.

Gratefulness
& Positive thoughts
are the only thing feeding
and fueling me!
Always remember that things can always be much worse.

Thank God for your path!

SHUNTONESE RICHARDSON

Letting God lead.
Let him use me.

PHASES OF A BUTTERFLY: THE CATERPILLAR

When I think about book one: the egg,
I think about how much life can change.

And how fast..

I'm no longer that girl anymore.
I'm shedding everything I used to be.
I'm not scared
or small.
I roam now.
I'm not new to this world,
anymore.

My future is getting clearer.
If I don't make the proper steps while being in this
caterpillar stage,
I won't make the cut.
My wings won't fly big and beautiful.

A lot of times
I wish I knew then,
What I know now.
But I guess that's the beauty of life.
You just have to keep on going
to keep on growing.

Use what you've been through
to get where you're going.

That's key.

PHASES OF A BUTTERFLY: THE CATERPILLAR

One of my biggest lessons learned during 2021
was controlling when to react to events that trigger me.

Now I'm working on not responding either.
Yes, there's a difference.
You react with action,
you respond with words.

When things bother me now,
I no longer react with my actions
But if words could kill,
I've always been the type to have the last word.
or even "make my point".
I'm mastering the idea,
that I don't care which side of the story anyone
other than I believe.

God knows my heart
and I don't have to say mean things
or explain myself with big think pieces
to sway other people to see my point of view.

Let who ever
Think whatever
As long as you're comfortable with your view.

SHUNTONESE RICHARDSON

"Results happen over time, not overnight."
So give yourself time.
You can't go from an egg to a butterfly in 24 hours.
It takes work,
patience,
Faith.
Like anything,
What you water will grow.
Give yourself a minute.

Believe that when the time is right,

YOUR WINGS WILL FLY!

Reminder of today:
….only the good things…..
Focus on them.
Appreciate them.
Bask in them.

Some days I don't know
how I'm doing it,
or what to do.

But I get it done.

PHASES OF A BUTTERFLY: THE CATERPILLAR

God is so good.
Win,
lose,
or draw.
I've always had God.
He's always had his hand in my mix.
Even when I was unaware of him being there.

When I was doing good,
I knew it was God.
And when I was doing bad,
I could still feel his presence.

08/26

I've been having chest pains for 8 days now.
Even though I pushed through my book club event,
because that's just what I do.
No excuses,
I'm the one who will always make it happen.
But who will make it happen in my absence
If I don't take care of my health?
Who will run my book club?
or my business?
If I don't start taking care of myself first?

I can't pour from an empty cup!

It's okay to say no
and rest.
It's okay to put the cup down
and just relax.

Selah.
I recently got this tattooed on me.
What a warning to myself.
I felt this Shut down coming all along.

Who will take care of my son
or run my errands?
If I overwork myself
and I'm dead
and gone?

Who will write my books?

Or go grocery shopping for my house?

Always putting my rest days on hold
or "until tomorrow"
because I don't want to feel unproductive.
Always looking for ways to stay busy
And getting things done.

Who will do these things if I don't take care of myself?
An overworked lady is not a wealthy lady.
Health is Wealth!
I think sometimes we forget that!

Less liquor,
More water.
More time for my health
and my body!

This body is the only one I have.
So if I want to be able to take care of
and save the world.

I SHOULD START TAKING CARE OF ME FIRST!

I had my first meeting with a real therapist today.
The session was 50 minutes
and it flew by.
I actually wished I had more time with her.
That's rare for me
because I don't trust easily.
We touched on that too.

How my trauma and my parents' actions
are affecting how I build relationships now.
That's the thing,
I don't.
I don't build new relationships.
I avoid letting new people in or even around me.

I'm not for the bullshit.

Even though I'm a social butterfly,
I only show what I'm comfortable showing.
Only the people around me
see the real me.

The vulnerable,
anxious,
control freak.
My negatives that sometimes ruin my days
but never push my friends away.
I can't see myself getting attached to people
and them leaving.

Today, even though it was my first session,

PHASES OF A BUTTERFLY: THE CATERPILLAR

my therapist said
"You don't know stability,
or security that's why you don't let people in"
And BOY did that hit it right on the head.

RIGHT NOW IS ABOUT STABILIZING.

Transparency is clear.
Blunt.
Straight forward.
Uncut.
Raw.
No matter how salty
or sweet
it may feel,
It's real.
Allowing yourself to feel.
That's a lot of strength.
So even if right now you're down
and/or hurting,

feel through it.

You'll get through it.

PHASES OF A BUTTERFLY: THE CATERPILLAR

Another Ramadhan down.
Another 30 days
Of fasting.
Of detox.
Weeding out unhealthy habits.
Strengthening my mind.
Ramadhan teaches you that if you can control
not eating for over 12 hours in a day,
No water.
No food,
No gum.
Nothing.
Then you can control your thoughts
And your mind

You can control anything.

Especially in your life.

That's hard core discipline.

"If they can scare you first,
they can get you to do anything." -JLT

That's how the military works.
They break down everything you've ever known
mentally,
physically,
emotionally

To build you up.

Stronger.
Wiser.
Disciplined.

If I'm not thankful for anything I've learned while serving
my country,
I learned self-control.
I learned time management.
I learned how to be a team and make decisions.

I'm a little rusty on following these concepts.
But I still have them in me.
They're still within.

Getting back to the Basics.
Red Phase if you will, battle.

PHASES OF A BUTTERFLY: THE CATERPILLAR

Watching Kanye's documentary is so inspiring.
I've gained a whole new love
and respect for him!
Despite other people
not believing in him,
he believed in himself
and his dreams.

This documentary backs everything I ever felt about myself.

As long as you have love
and at least one friend who believes in you
You can do anything
With God
and that mix,
you can't lose.

Stay disciplined.

You keep going,
you keep working.

You keep believing in YOU.

Assets.
4th quarter is always the hardest
but these goals on the vision boards aren't going to fill
and fulfill themselves!
Get planning,
get real!
Get it on paper.
The paper will pay your bills.

Start today!

The Girl Boss life isn't all keys
and big boxes of inventory!
Being a girl boss is hard!
There's so much to this life.
It's plumbing and lights.
It's HVAC.
And buying fans.
It's keeping it stocked and pretty.

You have to be the face,
the contractor
the painter
the interior designer
the driver
the worker
the planner
the graphics team
finance
and everything else.

You literally get no time for you!
No me time,
No mommy time,
No margaritas on a Tuesday.

Running on just E
and ideas!

But having a solid team makes it easier.
They make it worth it.

When running your businesses
if its is bigger than finances to you
it's bigger than anything this world can offer.

When you're doing what you love and genuinely staying
true to you, it just works.

And everyone around you can see it. They feel it.

One day, one of the girls in the shop, Niqua, said
"One of the main reasons I like this shop is the energy.
I've never seen you in a bad mood.
You always have a smile.
No matter what you got on your mind or dealing with,
you never let it affect how you interact with the team.
You are always coming in willing to help and fix any
problem we have.
Always making sure everyone is good."

And that,
that's what it's all about.

I give my businesses 100%.
Genuine and raw.
My feelings.
Emotions.
And ideas.

No matter the issue, I find solutions.
I keep God and my heart in it.
It makes a difference.

PHASES OF A BUTTERFLY: THE CATERPILLAR

I don't care about being perfect,
In business especially.
I don't wait until all my ducks are aligned,
I just crossed the street.
Sometimes you have to take what you have,
and make it work!
You'll learn and grow into where and who you want to be.

But for now,
give them what you got!

You can't say how your fight was or know what you
needed to improve on to win
If you don't get in the ring,

So use what you have right now and fight!

Don't ever let anyone make you feel weird for being yourself.
You're the only version of you this world is going to get.

Do what feels good,
to you.

Never let social media make you feel less
or undeserving of anything your heart desires.
Go for it all.

Nothing is too big.
Nothing is impossible.
It's okay to be the odd one out.
Or the one who is never on the scene.
It's okay to not fit in.

Find the people who fit with you and grow with them.

You can learn from every person you come across.
What you decide to keep
is up to you.
Inspiration is everywhere.

Always remain a student.
There's always something you can learn,
never get too big headed.
In anything
Life,
relationships,
friendships,
your businesses.
Always remain teachable.

Everywhere I go
I'm like a sponge,
I soak up as much knowledge as I can.
I never believed it was who you know,
But more of what you know.
Being knowledgeable in any skill set
or lane in this world and in this generation,
Will get you far and open many doors
.
Your knowledge will qualify you for rooms
you didn't even know you fit in.

At my book clubs annual boss brunch,
My friend and mentor Bishop stated that I was prolific.
Whenever I hear words I don't know I look them up.
So I stopped him and asked, what does that mean?

Prolific by sum of dictionary definition:
means plentiful.
Producing and productive.
In abundance.

He stated "Prolific means abundantly different,
extraordinary.
No other like you.
One of one"

Thankful for friends who speak power and love over me.
Now when people ask me about myself,
I have a new adjective to describe me.

I am prolific, obstinate and innovative.

Metamorphosis
"met·a·mor·pho·sis
/ˌmedəˈmôrfəsəs/
noun
•the process of transformation from an immature form to an adult form in two or more distinct stages.

•a change of the form or nature of a thing or person into a completely different one, by natural or supernatural means." Oxford Languages and Google

I read a quote that said
"Whatever you go
Out of God's light to abstain,
You have to stay out of His light to keep"

I no longer want anything
That's not in His image of me.

I want to be made in God's light.

PHASES OF A BUTTERFLY: THE CATERPILLAR

I have always used my platform to be transparent.
I always show the ups and the downs of getting to where I am.
I never left anything out.
Even the sour parts.

And sometimes, when life gives you no lemons,
You feel you have to take them.

The struggles of fighting your heart
because you know you're doing the wrong thing,
but you know you have to make a way
is hard.

Being the one who always makes a way
out of no way
is even harder.

Having a son to provide for alone
is one of the world's biggest struggles.
But struggling has shown me
that I don't have to be a statistic
and there is always a better way.

So before you make a decision
where you feel like you have no other option, your back is against the wall
and you do the wrong thing,
remember that you're not alone
and even in the dark
with your back against the wall

There's always a light.
You just have to find it.

Every time I get complacent
and content,
God shifts me.

My feelings are hurt,
my mind is jumbled.

I'm confused
and I'm tired.
I really just want to know what God wants for me.

Tomorrow is court day.
Today I'm learning to give myself grace.

I am not my mistakes
or my mishaps.
I am not the times I fell short
or made bad decisions.

I am still who God says I am.

GRACE

Move with Grace.
Love with Grace.
Give Grace.

To those around you who also fall short,
and most importantly,
Yourself!

Forgive yourself for all the times you fucked up.
Forgive yourself for not saying No.
Forgive yourself for sacrificing your livelihood for others.
Forgive yourself for letting loyalty make a fool of you.
Forgive yourself for feeding that greed with flesh and not
purity.

It's okay,
you fell.

Now get up.

Forgive you,

FIRST.

PHASES OF A BUTTERFLY: THE CATERPILLAR

I'm big on going with what I feel.

I remember months ago
I'd always tell my home girl
"a storm is coming".

A storm to me is a symbol for hardship.
The rain and lightning imagery for chaos and trauma.

And I was right.
My storm had come.

And now I'm finding cover during the rain and discomfort.

I'm wet, I'm scared, and in the open.
At any moment everything can come crashing down.

Uncertain of what's next.

RISK.

I've always been scared of the uncertainty of life.
Me and uncertainty,
don't get along.

Not knowing makes me uncomfortable.
But change is uncomfortable.
You only get uncomfortable when things are about to grow!

My wings are coming!

But how will I get to that stage of growth if I'm scared of change?

If I'm scared of taking the risk,
How will I ever know what being a butterfly truly feels like?

Certainty is an illusion.

PHASES OF A BUTTERFLY: THE CATERPILLAR

Only thing getting me through right now
is my grandmother's prayers.

People leave when the rain starts,
to run away from the storm

but they didn't know God was just watering your soul!

The flowers will come!
Don't get discouraged!
Let them go!

To my friends:
My go-tos.
For always sticking by me and having my back.
For holding my hand through the darkness.
For loving me when I couldn't love me.
For lending me your softness and realness.
For never telling my business or drama.
Thank you.

To Ranisha, my back bone.
Thanks for 10+ years of unconditional support.
Pregnancy,
sleeping in hotels with me,
Putting my socks on when I couldn't move my legs,
Writing me pages of letter when I was away in the
military without my phone,
holding me when I lost my brother and
Everything else you've seen me through.
We've been through everything together
and you've always been here.
Always and Forever the best of the best of friends.

To Latiyah, my other half.
The dark to my light,
pepper to my salt.
Iykyk- Batman & Robin.
Thank you for splitting $5 cheese sticks with me,
and our first 6 figure operations.
And still having the same loyalty and love that you did on
day 0.
I'll love and risk it all for you, for life.

To Devra,
My son's favorite TT and his other parent.
I literally never have to wonder
or worry about what will happen to Rahim
if things go wrong for me,
because I know you'd drop it all to be there for me and him.
One of the best big sisters I could have ever asked for.
My brain in most cases.

To Ndey,
My cooperate shawty.
The right to my wrong.
The one that makes my squiggly lines straight
and ideas just a little brighter.
My dreams are just a little bigger.

SHUNTONESE RICHARDSON

To Tiara,
We're opposite in every way,
but still one and the same.
For the days I couldn't get out of bed you would call me
every hour just to say "hey".
You don't know how many times you saved me.
Thanks for seeing the good in me.

To Adiaha,
My rider.
The one with the biggest heart
and the most love that I know will pull up first for any
problem,
with a solution.

PHASES OF A BUTTERFLY: THE CATERPILLAR

My sisters,
by choice that life handpicked perfectly for me.
I cry sometimes thinking about the obstacles
that just having a friend like you all
bring me through.
Appreciate each and every one of you
for having me time and time again.

I wouldn't be me without the love,
the words,
the prayers,
the support
or the laughs that carried me through all these years.

There's no way I can repay you
but I hope I'm just as valuable to you as you all are to me.

The mind leads
The body will follow.
Your brain will believe what you feed it.
Life is about what you water.
You really get out,
what you put in.
Everything comes full circle.

So do good.
Be good.

If you show love,
you get love.

And when you are a friend,
you make a couple of friends.
The real kind.
And that's the real tea on making and keeping solid friendships.

Kyia (part 2)
(Insider)
Do you guys just have that one person that just knows?
You never have to say too much
or explain how you feel…
they just know?
Even though she doesn't agree 95%
She's always right there.
Kinda like she can read my mind.
She just knows me.
My person.
My soulmate human.
I always feel understood.
Always feel heard.
Always felt.
Even when I'm annoying
and change my braid style
or come with my hair not combed out.
Thank you for letting me go to your house for weeks
so I can get to drill on time.
Thank you for driving me around at 8am before my book club meeting
to target to find a shirt.
Thank you for watching juju when I had to work.
Thank you for picking me up and sitting with me when
folks died and just letting me feel.
Thank you for always being my recharge.
Thank you for always being strict with your advice even
when I didn't ask you(lol)
Thank you for mixing patron and Hennessy with me
and always making sure I get home safe

SHUNTONESE RICHARDSON

and everything else you do for me!
You're one of the few people on earth who never irritate me.
And that alone is a reach.
I run to you when I feel my weakest.
Not for anything materialistic
but your presence.
Thanks for being you!
I love you.

PHASES OF A BUTTERFLY: THE CATERPILLAR

Working on yourself has its days.
2 weeks of ugly.
I relapsed.

The ugly truth is
we go back to our toxic ways
because they are not only what we are used to
but they are easier.

The harsh reality is
the only person holding us back from elevation
is us.
We often like to point fingers
and put the blame on anyone other than us
the reasons why things go wrong
but sometimes it's just us
to blame.

Sometimes I'm moody
and mean.
Sometimes I say things that are unforgivable.
Sometimes my actions push people away from me.

And that's my ugly truth.

I'm so afraid of people leaving me
or me looking weak
that I'm such an asshole sometimes that I self-sabotage.
Not even realizing that some people don't deserve the
harsh bullshit I really dish out.
And everybody is not going to deal with my mess.

And they don't have to.

As I'm distinguishing my own boundaries
I'm learning that others have boundaries of their own
in which they have to stand firm behind.
In which I have to respect.

I'm learning that I would prefer a partner who's attentive
and assertive.
A partner who will get down in my mess with me
after a shut down
and say
"what went wrong and how can we fix this".
I only want solutions based on love around me.

No one is perfect,
including me.
But I need people around
who are aware of our imperfections,
but willing enough to love each other
to who we want to be.

PHASES OF A BUTTERFLY: THE CATERPILLAR

Learning to love myself is teaching me how to love you.
I'm so grateful for the opportunity to be shown how I'm supposed to be loved.
So genuine
So pure
So innocent
You see no wrong in me
I'm mean,
Moody
And ugly…
But you still just love me.
Broken ole me.

I just push and push.
And yet,
You still love me.

You've shown me the meaning of unconditional love.
Sick
Single parent
Unhappy
Catching a federal case
Everything
You have seen me through it
And still loved me.

Hopefully I have enough time with you to fix myself
So I can be as perfect as you are to me..
But if I fall short and I'm too late
I'm just grateful I got to experience you in this world anyway.

Love is about composing.
Meeting your person on the level that they are on
and loving them in the language they can receive.

Unconditional
Without conditions.

A woman shouldn't have to go through trials and
tribulations
with a man
to prove to him
that she's worthy of love.

Let's kill that narrative.

When does being "understanding" turn into settling?

I've always been love.
I'll always be love.
I'm not changing that
for nothing.
I'm not changing me
for nothing.
No matter how many times I'm left
or let down.
I'll remain me.
To my purest form.

PHASES OF A BUTTERFLY: THE CATERPILLAR

You know how people feel when they see butterflies?
Lucky?
Blessed?

Butterfly treatment or leave me alone.

Today my therapist said
"Before you respond to things, take a minute and breathe."
and I'll say "usually I'll snap back ok you, but I'm working on something different"
and I felt that.
Learning and accepting that I can't control other people's actions
but I can
I should
and will start controlling how I respond
and the energy I give!

I used to be so nervous to talk to a therapist
but now I look forward to speaking with her every week.
This week, I even wanted two sessions.

I love having someone to confide in
who isn't judgmental
but is trained enough to read through my cluttered life
and tell me how I can fix myself.

I love this for me.

If you're looking for a sign to talk to someone
this is it.

Here's to the girls not scared of healing or working on themselves!

It takes boatloads of courage!

PHASES OF A BUTTERFLY: THE CATERPILLAR

Being a black woman in America,

You have to be twice as good.
Twice as smart.
Twice as strong.

CONFIRMED:
Judge Ketanji Brown Jackson to the Supreme Court,
making her the 116th justice
and the first Black woman
to serve on the top U.S. court.

The feeling is overwhelming.
I'm so proud.

Anytime I see a black woman in the media,
I'm reminded that we are love.
That we are light.
That WE can do anything!

I am my ancestors' wildest dreams.

PHASES OF A BUTTERFLY: THE CATERPILLAR

Serena Williams.
Venus Williams.
Michelle Obama.
Sandra Bland.
Rosa Parks.
Angela Davis.
Billie Holiday.
Harriet Tubman.
Coretta Scott King.
Oprah Winfrey.
Sha'carri Richardson.
Kentanji Brown.
Maya Angelou.
Breonna Taylor.
Sonority Truth.

Shuntonese Richardson

SHUNTONESE RICHARDSON

I'm not cocky,
I'm filled with God's love

I'm confident, it's a difference.

PHASES OF A BUTTERFLY: THE CATERPILLAR

Sarah Jake's always turns my day around.
Today I listened to one called
"Getting the most out life"
and at first I was not going to watch it
I was going to watch another one
but this one called my name.

In this scripture she talked about MORE.
And how some may not be asking for more
and are content with what they have.

But God had dropped more upon us.

And it feels heavy.
It feels overwhelming.
It feels like a lot.

That's me.

I'm stressed
and I'm tired.

But now I'm understanding that it's because God is
assigning more to me
because He believes in me.

So no more asking 'why me'
and more 'why not me'.

I'm that good.
I'm over qualified.

I deserve this.

No more letting doubt cloud my judgment regarding me.
No more letting worry of who I used to be or the storm

stop me from becoming who God has called me to be.

PHASES OF A BUTTERFLY: THE CATERPILLAR

I'll never count myself out.

I know.
I know what it looks like.
I know what it looked like in the news.
I see what the article said.
I heard what the people whispered.
I heard what the prosecutors alleged.
I heard what the family thinks......

but God.

GOD SAID HE AIN'T THROUGH WITH ME YET.

And He gets the last say-so-on me.

I can't believe I'm about to be 25.
The feeling is weird.
When I was a young girl
I dreamed of how my life would look
at 25.
Quarter century.
Thinking about that little girl
and comparing her to me right now…

She'd be so proud.
I'm so proud.
I've accomplished so much in my 25 laps.

I've fallen more times
than I've won,
to me.
But I count them all.

I'm not far from who I've imagined me to be
and I'm grateful for that.
I pictured a fancy car, a salon and a husband,
lol yeah right.

I guess I'm 75% there.
I'll take that!

Hold the husband,
Thanks God.

I feel so grown, thinking about 25.
Only one more year left on my mom's insurance.

Like I'm supposed to be somewhere else.
But I feel so content.
Because I know I'm exactly where I'm supposed to be.

I'm not scared
but I'm always anxious.
I'm calculating my moves more now than I've ever been.

Because my mistakes in previous years
have changed many things for me.

But I'm not scared.
I'll face 25,
with the same heart I've faced the other 24.

Chance,
changes and all.
I'll use my Witt,
my faith,
and my heart
to get me to another 25.

Your fullest potential hasn't been reached but we're working.
You still have a long way to go and while the journey is tough,
It's still beautiful.
Don't give up.
Give yourself time to become a butterfly.

PHASES OF A BUTTERFLY: THE CATERPILLAR

"If you can't find the light
be the light.
If you can't find the love
be the love"

About the author

Shuntonese Richadson is a 2x self-published author and owner of SNR Publishing where she mentors others to self-publish and start businesses. She is also the owner of The SNR Collection Boutique and Beauty Bar and founder of Bookd the book club, a non-profit both located in Chicago Il. She's been to school to become a Licensed Esthetician and has her Associates degree in Criminal Justice. She is a prolific boy mom, a veteran and serial entrepreneur.

Follow and Grow with the author:

www.thesnrcollection.com

Instagram:
@thesnrcollection_
@thesnrpublishingco
@bookdthebookclubnfp

www.ingramcontent.com/pod-product-compliance
Lightning Source LLC
Chambersburg PA
CBHW072014290426
44109CB00018B/2232